PIANO • VOCAL • GUITAR

THE MAMAS AND THE PAPAS

A Publication of

MCA
music publishing
A Division of MCA Inc.
7777 West Bluemound Road Milwaukee, Wisconsin 53213
Exclusively Distributed by
Hal Leonard Publishing Corporation

ISBN 0-7935-0836-3

THE MAMAS AND THE PAPAS

The History of

"All the leaves are brown and the sky is grey....I'd be safe and warm, if I was in L.A...." It was January of 1962. John Phillips and his wife-to-be, Michelle Gilliam, had just arrived in New York from California. "We were staying in the Earl Hotel off Washington Square," recalls John. "It was Michelle's first time East. She was 18 at the time. One morning we woke up and she said, 'What's going on, what's going on?' And I said, 'It's snowing Michelle.'

"She says,'SNOWING?' She had never seen snow in her life. Really the California Girl Brian Wilson wrote about.

"So we went for a walk that day, and she had no winter clothes and got chilled to the bone. Along the way we stopped in a church and got warm. We kept thinking about California's bright sun and blue sky...."

Four years later, the song that came out of Michelle's first snow storm launched the Mamas and the Papas on a fast and hard-burning ride to stardom. With its sunny, close-knit harmonies, its easy, folk-rock rhythm, and its promise of greener pastures, "California Dreamin'" was released on Dunhill Records in November, '65 and climbed to the the No. 4 slot in early 1966. Almost overnight, songwriters John and Michelle, a honey-toned lead tenor named Denny Doherty, and a free-wheeling, gutsy alto who called herself Cass Elliot had blossomed from down-and-out, sweet-singing hippies to high rolling superstars. As Jay Lasker, one of Dunhill's three principals, would later comment to *Forbes* magazine, "These four animals walked right in off the street."

"They were such a motley looking group," recalls drummer extraordinare Hal Blaine of his first sessions with them in the summer of '65 at L.A.'s Western studios. Blaine, along with bassist Joe Osborne and keyboardist Larry Knechtel, would eventually play on all the Mamas and Papas big records. "But the minute John started singing 'California Dreamin',' we knew a major hit was in the making."

Like most overnight success stories, the Mamas and the Papas breakthrough had been a long time in coming. John, the group's primary songwriter and musical mastermind, was 31 when "California Dreamin'" took off, and, like Cass and Denny, had long been laboring in the folk-music trenches. His checkered career dates back to a high school street gang in Alexandria, Virginia called the Del Ray Locals. "We sang lamppost harmony—doo wop stuff," he says. "We'd sit around the playground till one or two in the morning harmonizing 'Earth Angel.'" The Del Ray Locals begat the Abstracts, a folk-jazz quartet whose trademark tune in 1959 was "How High the Moon."

"We wore crewcuts, blazers, and little matching outfits," says Phillips. "We worked locally, and we kept driving up to New York and knocking on doors at the Brill Building."

Musically, John modelled the Abstracts on the harmonies of the Four Lads, and the open sound and freely moving parts of the Hi-Lo's, the Four Freshmen, and the Four Aces. "I loved the wide open voicings," he says, "with the sixth of the chord on the bottom. I learned a lot from listening to them. I was also influenced by the Kingston Trio and the Clancy Brothers."

In 1960, the Abstracts became the Smoothies, and lead tenor Phil Blondheim changed his name to Scott McKenzie, after the middle name of Laura Mackenzie Phillips, John's newborn daughter by Susie, whom he had married in 1957. The Smoothies landed a contract with

Decca and recorded John's "Softly," a lushly orchestrated ballad that fit right into the current musical climate — Percy Faith's "Theme from *A Summer Place*" was the No. 1 record of the year. "Softly" didn't generate much chart action, but it did land the Smoothies on Dick Clark's *American Bandstand*, where they shared the bill with Conway Twitty.

A year later, Phillips and Scott McKenzie abandoned the Smoothies to form the folk group the Journeymen with Dick Weissman. "Dick was our resident musicologist," says Phillips. "He knew folk music inside out—all the Lomax series, the Southern heritage." With McKenzie's smooth vocals, John's commercial songwriting skills, and Weissman's unparalleled musicianship and knowledge of the folk repertoire, the Journeymen took off. By 1963, they had recorded three albums for Capitol.

Among their earliest dates, in April '61, was Gerde's Folk City, where they were featured alongside Bob Dylan; perhaps their most significant engagement, however, also in '61, was L.A.'s Hungry i, a hot night spot frequented by a 17-year-old part-time model named Michelle Gilliam.

The attraction was strong, immediate, and mutual. Gilliam was young, spirited, and beautiful. Phillips, eight years her senior, was a successful songwriter and part of the San Francisco elite. Each saw in the other something worth pursuing. Within a year, Phillips had divorced Susie to be with Michelle.

The couple came east, where she began modeling in earnest and he became immersed in the Greenwich Village folk scene with the Journeymen. ("California Dreamin'," written during this time, was originally conceived as a folksong, though John never performed it that way publicly.) In 1963, the Journeymen were booked on a hootenanny tour along with Glenn Yarbrough of the Limelighters and a Canadian group called the Halifax Three, whose lead singer was Denny Doherty. "We were thrown together in a package deal," says Doherty. "We were touring the south. At the same time Cass was in the Big 3 touring the north."

Ultimately, Doherty left the Halifax Three to join with Cass, Zal Yanovsky, and Jim Hendricks to form Cass Elliot and the Big 3. Then they added a drummer and called themselves the Mugwumps, making one album's worth of material for Warner Bros. Records. John Sebastian was one of their sidemen, and he and Yanovsky went on to form the Lovin' Spoonful.

By the spring of '64, McKenzie and Weissman had left the Journeymen. But Phillips wasn't ready to quit the folk scene quite yet. He convinced Michelle, by now his wife, to take voice lessons, joined up with a hot banjo picker named Marshall Brickman, and created the New Journeymen. All he needed was a lead vocalist.

"The Beatles had invaded," recalls Doherty. "The Mugwumps had broken up. Cass and Yanovsky and I were all back in New York, living at the Albert Hotel. No one had a job, the bills needed to be paid, and the management was threatening to throw us out. The phone rings and it's John, saying he remembers me from the hootenanny tour and wants to put together the New Journeymen with Michelle. They had a date at the Shoreham Hotel in Washington, so over the weekend, I had to learn 28 songs." The new folk group was a success, playing at the Shoreham as the warmup act for Bill Cosby.

But the folk scene was fading fast, and so was the trio's enthusiasm for it. It was time for a change. Armed with their New Journeymen earnings and an American Express Card, Doherty and the Phillipses headed for the Virgin Islands, complete with dogs and a five-year-old Laura Mackenzie Phillips in tow. Cass eventually followed them, primarily to be with Doherty. ("Cass and I had a very strange relationship," he reports, "She wanted my parts.")

They lived on the beach in pup tents, dropped acid, and sang "California Dreamin'," "Go Where You Wanna Go" and "I Saw Her Again," the last two of which John wrote, he says, in response to Michelle's wandering eye. Gradually, Cass began to sing with them. "At first," says Michelle, "John didn't really want her in the group because she was so independent, and because her voice didn't really blend that well. But the more she sang with us, the more it became apparent that that's where the sound was."

John says he changed his mind about Cass when her voice changed: "She had always been about two tones too low for my arrangements," explains John. "She just couldn't get there. Michelle has a very high voice. Sort of a coloratura. I needed a really strong alto. Cass's sound was perfect but the range was wrong." Then one day, while wandering around a construction site, Cass was hit by a copper pipe. "She was in the hospital for about three days with a concussion," says John. "I don't know if her sinuses cleared or what, but her voice got higher. It was just what we needed."

As the quartet honed its sound, the local authorities became less and less enamored of the free-wheeling antics on the beach. "We finally split when the governor threw us off the island," says Doherty. By that time they were completely broke. "We wound up living with Cass in L.A. in a crash pad with eviction notices posted on the door," says Denny.

In California, they ran into their old friend from the Christy Minstrels, Barry McGuire. He had just had a huge hit with "Eve of Destruction." On hearing the fruits of his friends' musical labors, he offered to introduce them to his producer, Lou Adler. Along with Jay Lasker and Bobby Roberts, Adler was one of the principals of a small, independent label named Dunhill. Adler found and produced the talent, Roberts managed it, and Lasker promoted and sold it.

It was the summer of '65, and out of the car radio blared the Stones' "Satisfaction," the Beach Boys' "California Girls," and the Beatles "Help." Dunhill was looking for a follow-up hit to McGuire's and in walked this motley crew with "California Dreamin'," "Monday Monday," "Go Where You Wanna Go," and "I Saw Her Again."

Adler was thrilled with what he heard. As Doherty recalls it, "Lou said, 'I'll give you whatever you want—just don't go see anybody else.' And John replied with his best line ever: 'Lou, what we want is a steady stream of money from your office to our house. We don't have a house yet, and if we did, we couldn't get there, because we don't have a car.' So we wound up with cash, a house, a car, and 'California Dreamin' in the can."

Initially, Adler signed the group to sing backup vocals on McGuire's new LP, *This Precious Time*, one of whose cuts was "California Dreamin.'" "We did the backgrounds and Barry sang lead," recalls John. "And then Lou asked, 'Couldn't Denny sing that song, John?' I said, 'Sure, but it'd have to be an octave higher.' We were a little

worried about hurting Barry's feelings, so we both recorded it." The two recordings use exactly the same instrumental and backup-vocal tracks. But Doherty's lead vocal made the song a commercial success.

The single was released in November, 1965. "Just 19 weeks after we recorded it." says Doherty, "it came on the charts at 40 with a bullet. David Crosby [then of the Byrds] stopped me on the street and said, 'Congratulations!' I didn't know what he was talking about."

Dunhill released the first album, **If You Can Believe Your Eyes And Ears—The Mamas And The Papas** (as they now called themselves) in January of '66, with "California Dreamin'" at the height of its popularity. The kinky album cover with the four of them in a bathtub said it all: This was something completely different. First of all, most groups of the time were either all male or all female. This one not only featured a mixed timbre, but great tunes with unusual voicings and fresh harmonies. Folk-rock with a twist. *Life* magazine called them "...the most inventive pop musical group and first really new vocal sound since the Beatles." Indeed, in the wake of the British invasion, it was the Mamas and the Papas, along with groups like the Byrds and Buffalo Springfield, who ultimately brought the focus back to America.

The followup to "California Dreamin" was "Monday, Monday," which, much to the amazement of Michelle and Cass, became the quartet's biggest record ever. "I told John I thought 'Monday,

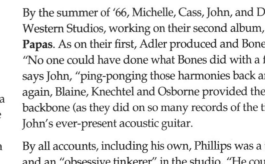

Monday' was so contrived," says Michelle. "I didn't like the lyric. I wasn't crazy about the melody. John loved it. Denny loved it. Lou loved it. Cass and I hated it. When Lou said it would be our next song, the two of us went to him and said, 'This is a terrible idea. It will be the end of what was to be a great career for all of us.' Then it raced up the charts and became a No. 1 single." Ultimately it also earned them a Grammy for "Best Contemporary Rock & Roll Performance" of 1966.

By this time, Cass and Michelle, despite their vast differences in size and style, were fast friends. "Cass was the first real emancipated woman I ever knew,"says Michelle. "She had an enormous effect on me, both personally and musically. In the beginning, the only singing I'd ever done was in a Baptist church. Cass was always trying to get me to sing a little more on the bluesy side than on the Quaker side. She gave me the confidence to sing things I didn't think I could. She'd say,'Well come on, we'll sing it together. If you don't hit the note, I will."

"Cass was a great influence on her," concurs John, "because Cass was such a natural singer. She had real street smarts when it came to music."

By the summer of '66, Michelle, Cass, John, and Denny were back at Western Studios, working on their second album, **The Mamas And The Papas**. As on their first, Adler produced and Bones Howe engineered. "No one could have done what Bones did with a four-track machine," says John, "ping-ponging those harmonies back and forth." And once again, Blaine, Knechtel and Osborne provided the album's instrumental backbone (as they did on so many records of the time), topped off by John's ever-present acoustic guitar.

By all accounts, including his own, Phillips was a taskmaster in rehearsal and an "obsessive tinkerer" in the studio. "He could prod you gently or kick you in the ass," says Michelle. "He'd say, 'You've got to hit that note, and I mean it—hit it on the next take.' He made you do things you never thought you were capable of doing. I would never have accomplished the things I did musically without John's encouragement and insistence."

They rehearsed constantly. "I'd write the song and get the group together with one 12-string guitar to work out the feel and harmony parts I wanted," says John. "The test for me was if it sounded great in the living room with one guitar, once you got into the studio it'd be really hot."

The second album spawned the hit singles, "Words of Love," "I Saw Her Again Last Night," and "Dancing in the Street," which Martha and the Vandellas had popularized three years earlier.

By this time, the cash flow problems of the Greenwich Village folk scene were long gone. John and Michelle purchased the Jeanette MacDonald mansion in Bel Air, Doherty moved into a 14-room palace in Laurel Canyon, and Elliot found her dream house in Nichols Canyon, right next door to Rudy Vallee.

"It was crazy," says John. "We were overnight millionaires. No one had a chance to grasp the meaning of it. We just rented planes and bought clothes." And partied. The soirees in the Bel Air mansion, attended by the Beach Boys, Tommy Smothers, Jane Fonda, Jack Nicholson, and other luminaries, are legend. The Mamas and the Papas were having so much fun at home that, by John's estimate, in the two-and-a-half years the group was together, they played only 30 concerts.

"The tours never worked anyway," he says. "We always lost money. The room service bill would be eight billion dollars, and Cass would invite the entire city of Chicago to breakfast."

Their free-wheeling persona was precisely what appealed to such a diverse record-buying public. The Mamas and the Papas were frequent guests of **Ed Sullivan, Shindig,** the **Hollywood Palace with Arthur Godfrey,** and of course **American Bandstand.** Cass, usually clad in a tent dress and suede boots, was the personality behind the group—the natural, outgoing earth mother who was so easy for an audience to warm to; Michelle was the cool, sexy one ("I may have looked cool," she says today, "but I was just plain terrified"), frequently seen in long, close-fitting garb and rarely cracking a smile; Denny, ever the devilish Irishman, favored Nehru jackets and a perpetual "out there" look; John wore his guitar and a friendly but somewhat awkward demeanor, as if he didn't really mean to be six-foot-four.

It all looked like so much fun. But, inevitably, there were problems. Michelle and Denny had an affair, which took its toll on her marriage to John, on her friendship with Cass, and on Cass's longtime love for Denny. "It got to be impossible for Michelle and me to be on the same side of the street, much less in the same studio," says John. "It was crazy." His solution was to fire her from the group. In the summer of '66, Michelle received a formal letter from Dunhill stating, "your services are no longer required...." She was devastated.

Jill Gibson, Lou Adler's girlfriend and a Michelle lookalike, was brought in for several months as a replacement. Michelle was finally asked back, but things were never quite the same again.

The third album, **The Mamas And The Papas Deliver**, came out in '67 and contained "Creeque Alley" a delightful documentation of the group's history ("John and Michie were gettin' kind of itchie just to leave the folk music behind... And no one's gettin' fat except Mama Cass") and a version of the Shirelles' 1961 hit, "Dedicated To The One I Love," which the Mamas and the Papas had long used as a vocal warmup before their live concerts.

That summer was the Monterey Pop Festival, of which John and Michelle were primary organizers. Janis Joplin, Simon and Garfunkel, the Who, Jimi Hendrix, Ravi Shankar and the Jefferson Airplane all performed, as did Scott McKenzie, singing the festival's anthem, "San Francisco (Be Sure to Wear Flowers in Your Hair)," which John had written for him. That spring, Cass had given birth to her daughter, Owen Vanessa, refusing to divulge the father's name, yet thrilled with her new motherhood role.

Album four, **The Papas And The Mamas**, was recorded in the Bel Air mansion studio in 1968. Charting singles included "Twelve Thirty,"

"For the Love of Ivy," "Safe in My Garden," and "Dream a Little Dream of Me," the first single released under Cass' own name and the beginning of her solo career. In retrospect, the number of hits the Mamas and Papas had generated in just under three years was phenomenal. Phillips is clearly one of the most prolific and inventive musical minds of a generation.

In the fall of '68, the Mamas and the Papas sailed to England on the SS France to play London's Royal Albert Hall. But, when Cass was arrested (on what proved to be false charges) while disembarking, they quickly cancelled. After nearly three years, it was all getting to be too much. Michelle, pregnant with daughter Chynna (Phillips of Wilson Phillips), was still smarting from the firing, and she and John fought frequently; Denny had been drifting further and further away; and Cass was itching to pursue her solo act. They decided to call it quits.

Cass went off on her own, ultimately recording albums for Dunhill and RCA Records, and playing the club scene, including Caesar's Palace in Las Vegas. A popular TV personality, she hosted **The Tonight Show** no less than a dozen times, and had her own television show, **Don't Call Me Mama Anymore**. ("She always hated being called Mama Cass," says Michelle.)

John and Michelle were finally divorced in 1970, the same year John released his solo LP, **John The Wolfking Of L.A.**, which he calls "an instant collector's item." Michelle went on to pursue an acting career, and in 1977 released her solo disc, **Victim of Romance**, which did about as well as John's. Denny's solo effort, **Watcha Gonna Do**, came out in 1971.

Meanwhile, back in the corporate offices. Dunhill—now owned by ABC—claimed the group still owed them one more recording. So John set about putting together a reunion LP in 1970. "By that time, everyone was so nuts, from LSD, lifestyle, and everything else," he says, "we had all scattered to the four corners of the world; I never had all four of them in the studio at the same time. I worked for almost a year, catching people as they went through town to teach them a part, and then overdubbing it on tape. Cass had her own private nurse who was constantly taking her blood pressure. It was horrible—totally opposite from the way we had always worked so closely in the past." ABC issued **People Like Us** in 1971. It was their final group effort.

Two years later, Cass died of a heart attack in England. "She had finally come into her own," says Denny. "She was on the verge of having it all, and away it went." The world was stunned by her death. Some of the news media claimed it was drug-related, others that she had choked on a ham sandwich. John says it was neither, that between her weight and all the hard living, her heart just simply gave out.

Today, the three Mamas and Papas are each flourishing. Denny is living in Toronto, writing songs and acting in theater; Michelle is in Los Angeles, where her thriving screen career includes playing Ann Mattheson on **Knot's Landing**. ("I'm the mother from hell," she says with pride.) And John, having quit the drug scene, is living on Long Island and touring with a new incarnation of the Mamas and the Papas that he put together in 1981. Daughter Mackenzie Phillips sings Michelle's parts, Elaine "Spanky" McFarlane sings Cass'; and Scott McKenzie sings lead, having replaced Denny in that role in 1987.

The new Mamas and the Papas tour internationally, singing all the old songs. "It's just amazing," says John, "because people all over the world know every word—even young kids. We just stop singing and put the microphones out there, and they keep right on going." And so does the legacy of one of our generation's most original and kaleidoscopically colorful pop quartets.—Susan Elliot

CALIFORNIA DREAMIN'

Words and Music by JOHN PHILLIPS
and MICHELLE PHILLIPS

MCA music publishing

CREEQUE ALLEY

Words and Music by JOHN PHILLIPS
and MICHELLE GILLIAM

1. John and Mitch - ie were get - tin' kind of itch - y just to leave the folk mu - sic be - hind.__ Let's go __ south."

2. - ly said, "Den - ny, you know __ there aren't man - y who can sing a song the way that you do. __ Den - ny says, "Zal - ly, gol - ly,

3.-5. *See additional lyrics*

Zal and Den - ny work -

MCA music publishing

9

Additional Lyrics

3. When Cass was a sophomore,
   planned to go to Swarthmore,
   but she changed her mind one day.
   Standin' on the turnpike
   thumb out to hitchhike,
   take her to New York right away.
   When Denny met Cass he gave her love bumps,
   called John and Zal and that was the Mugwumps.
   McGuinn and McGuire couldn't get no higher,
   but that's what they were aimin' at,
   and no one's gettin' fat except Mama Cass.

4. Mugwumps, high jumps, slow slumps, big bumps.
   Don't you work as hard as you play?
   Make-up, break-up, ev'rything you shake up,
   guess it had to be that way.
   Sebastian and Zal formed a Spoonful;
   Michelle, John and Denny gettin' very tuneful.
   McGuinn and McGuire just a-catchin' fire.
   In L.A. you know where that's at.
   And everybody's gettin' fat except Mama Cass.
   Do do do do do do, do do do do, woh.

5. Broke, busted, disgusted, agents can't be trusted;
   and then she wants to go to the sea.
   Cass can't make it. She says, "We'll have to fake it."
   We knew she'd come eventually.
   Greasin' on American Express card,
   Tents, low rent and keepin' out the heat's hard
   Duffy's good vibrations and our imaginations
   can't go on indefinitely,
   and California Dreamin' is becoming a reality.

DANCING IN THE STREET

Words and Music by WILLIAM STEVENSON,
MARVIN GAYE and IVY HUNTER

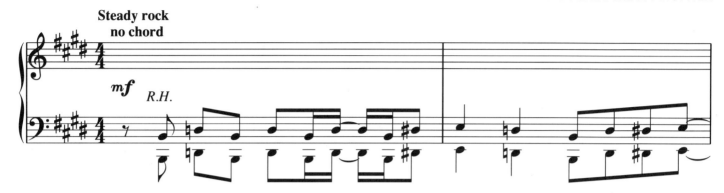

Call - ing out _ a round _ the world, "Are you
in - vi - ta - tion a - cross the na - tion, a

read - y for a brand new beat?" Sum-mer's here, __ and the
chance_ for the folks to meet. _____ There'll be laugh-ing, _ sing - ing, and

time is right ____ for danc - ing ___ in the streets. __
mu - sic swing - ing and danc - ing ___ in the streets. __

__ They're danc - ing in ___ Chi - ca - go, ___
__ Phil - a - del - phia P. A., ___

down in New Or - leans, __
Balt - i - more and D. C., ___ now, ___

Phil - a - del-phia P. A., ___
Instrumental - Spoken ad lib. names of cities

Balt - i -more and D. C. ___ now, ___

And if we get ___ to that Mo - tor Cit - y, Ah, _

Repeat and Fade

___ way down ___ in L. A., Cal - i - for - ni - a.

DEDICATED TO THE ONE I LOVE

Words and Music by LOWMAN PAULING
and RALPH BASS

DREAM A LITTLE DREAM OF ME

Words by GUS KAHN
Music by WILBUR SCHWANDT & FABIAN ANDRE

Stars shin-ing bright a - bove you,

Night breez-es seem to whis-per, "I love you," Birds sing-ing in the

syc - a - more tree, "Dream a lit - tle dream of me."

GLAD TO BE UNHAPPY

Words by LORENZ HART
Music by RICHARD RODGERS

GO WHERE YOU WANNA GO

Words and Music by
JOHN PHILLIPS

do what you wan-na do __ with whom - ev - er you wan-na do __ it, babe. __

You don't un - der - stand __ that a girl like me can love __

__ just one man. __

Three thou - sand miles, __ that's how far you'll
You've been gone a week __ and I've tried so

GOT A FEELIN'

Words and Music by JOHN PHILLIPS
and DENNIS DOHERTY

Gently, with a beat

1.,3. Got a feel - ing that __ I'm wast - ing time _____ on
2. Got a feel - ing that __ your play - ing some game _____ with

you, _____ babe. _ Got a feel - ing that __ you've been un - true. _
me, _____ babe. _ Got a feel - ing that __ you just can't see. _

I CALL YOUR NAME

Words and Music by JOHN LENNON
and PAUL McCARTNEY

I SAW HER AGAIN LAST NIGHT

Words and Music by JOHN PHILLIPS
and DENNIS DOHERTY

MCA music publishing

MY GIRL

Words and Music by WILLIAM "SMOKEY" ROBINSON
and RONALD WHITE

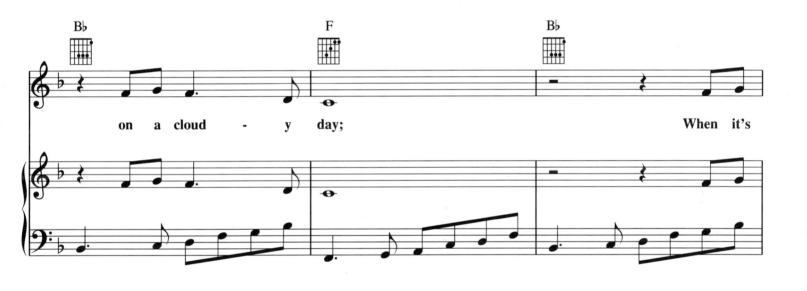

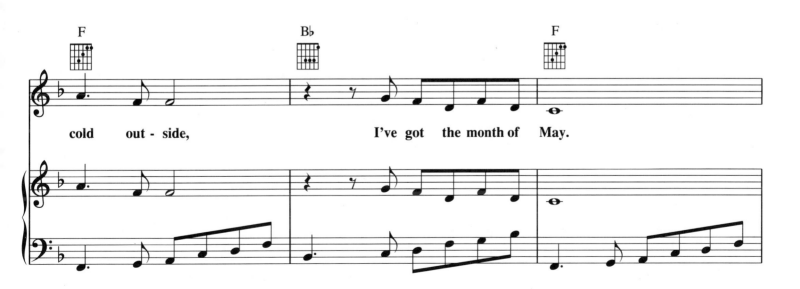

LOOK THROUGH MY WINDOW

Words and Music by
JOHN PHILLIPS

MCA music publishing

MIDNIGHT VOYAGE

Words and Music by
JOHN PHILLIPS

MONDAY, MONDAY

Words and Music by JOHN PHILLIPS

Moderately

MCA music publishing

WORDS OF LOVE

Words and Music by
JOHN PHILLIPS

MCA music publishing

TWELVE-THIRTY
(YOUNG GIRLS ARE COMING TO THE CANYON)

Words and Music by
JOHN PHILLIPS